UNLOCKING THE HARVEST WITHIN YOU

E. A. EFFIOM

PUBLISHERS OF INSPIRATION

Copyright © 2012 E. A Effiom

All rights reserved. No part of this publication may be produced, distributed, or transmitted in any form or by any means, including photocopying, recording, or other electronic or mechanical methods, without the prior written permission of the publisher, except in the case of brief quotations embodied in critical reviews and certain other noncommercial uses permitted by copyright law.

For permission requests, write to the publisher, addressed "Attention: Permissions Coordinator" at the email address below:

Ministry In Art Media Ltd

e-mail: info@miapublishing.com

www.miapublishing.com

Unless otherwise stated, all scripture quotations are taken from the Holy Bible, New King James Version. Quotations marked NKJV are taken from the HOLY BIBLE, NEW KING JAMES VERSION. Copyright © 1973, 1978, 1984 by International Bible Society. Used by permission of Hodder and Stoughton Ltd, a member of the Hodder Headline Plc Group. All rights reserved. "NKJV" is a registered trademark of International Bible Society. UK trademark number 1448790.

Quotations marked KJV are from the Holy Bible,

King James Version.

ISBN Number: 978-1-907402-37-1

Cover Design: Allan Sealy

Contents

Acknowledgements 7

Forward 9

Preface 13

1. The Million Dollar Gem in You 17

2. Your "Garden House" 21

3. Living Involves Challenges 27

4. Essential Reminders 35

5. Unleash Your Faith 59

6. Authentic Relationships Are Important 73

7. From 'Little' To 'Much'. 83

8. Self – Discipline. 101

9. The Power Of Your Decisions. 111

10. Ten Practical Steps To Help
    Unlock Your Own Harvest. 119

11. 5 Things You Should
    Know About Harvest 127

12. Last Word. 147

✽

Dedication

I dedicate this book to my father, Teacher Effiom, the first Preacher I ever listened to and my mother, Ma Effiom, both of whom modelled the life I have grown to live and love as a Christian. I recall at age 6 overhearing dad pray that God should anoint at least one of his children to preach The Gospel like him. Thank you.

※

Acknowledgements

There is absolutely no way this book would have been possible without the support and contribution of many. Pastor Edak, my dear wife and closest friend, my confidante, you persisted in telling me there are books in me. Your love and support is invaluable. Thank you for reading through and editing the script. To my dear children and fellow ministers, Vickie, Steph and David, you guys are outstanding and I love you all very much.

My special thanks also to my dear brothers and sisters and their families. Your love and support for me through the journey of life and Ministry will never be forgotten. Thank you.

Thank you, Pastor Aity Inyang and your staff, for transcribing the initial material.

The wonderful members of Nu – Life Church, London, are the very best any pastor could ask for. Thank you for believing in me as your pastor. I love each and every one of you very much.

My special appreciation goes to Pastors Tony and Shola Peters, my dear friends, who made the time to read through the script and very kindly wrote the forward to this book. Your counsel has been immensely helpful. You are valued friends.

✶

Forward

Now to Him who is able to do exceedingly abundantly above all that we ask or think, according to the power that works in us, to Him be glory in the church by Christ Jesus to all generations, forever and ever. Amen.
(Ephesians 3:20-21.)

Life invariably comes with its share of challenges and setbacks. Nevertheless, God has placed in every one of His children, a supernatural resource to help us deal effectively, wisely and courageously with every challenging situation we face.

If we don't realise or believe that this divine potential is in us, we will struggle through life and feel like victims. On the other hand, when we discover and deploy the unlimited power within us, we will attack all of life with faith and godly confidence.

'Unlocking the Harvest within' will show you clearly and scripturally, that you have all you need in Christ to live life to the fullest. It will also help you see that the victories and breakthroughs you desire can start from what you already have in your possession.

In this highly readable book, Rev. E A Effiom, takes us on a journey of faith coupled with personal responsibility. He shows us how to appreciate the 'little' things we take for granted in life; how to dwell on what we have, not on what we don't have; and how to faithfully use what we have before we start exercising our faith for bigger things.

If, like the rest of us, you've ever felt inadequately equipped for the tasks and challenges ahead of

Forward

you, 'Unlocking the Harvest within' will give you perspective, hope and courage. It will challenge you to embrace a Christ-centred life and connect to the limitless power at work in you.

– Rev. Tony Peters,
Senior Pastor, **The King's House**
London's Alive Church

✷

Preface

I once saw a documentary on Television about a lady Truck driver. She was truly a tough woman. She drove one of those huge vehicles that deliver goods right across the length and breadth of the America. Imagine the distance they cover, and the lifestyles they have to get used to. You must have the heart for it. They do go sometimes for weeks on the road, only resting at designated places etc.

On one of her many journeys, this lady found herself in a small town, and since she had some time on her hands, she went into the local street market. She found a painting which she liked and the seller was all too glad to let it go for $5. Quite a bargain!

There was no need for a receipt; after all it was only worth a fiver.

The beautiful painting was left in the cabin of the truck for very many years, until the lady was clearing out her vessel one last time, as she was retiring from the highways due to age. Once retired, she now had time to watch TV at home and rest her body from the long years of hard work.

That was when she watched a program about popular artists and their paintings that cost hundreds of thousands of dollars, and some very special ones, going for millions of dollars. Out of curiosity, she located where she had dumped her 'painting' under the bed in the guest room. She brought it out and dusted it and then decided to take it to a nearby arts gallery for valuation, "Who knows?" she thought to herself!

The Director of the gallery took one look at the painting, then a second look and requested her to allow him a few moments to run some tests. After about an hour, he came out from his inner office and told the anxious lady, that there was a chance it could be a painting by one of the masters, 'Jonathan Pollock', but he was almost definitely sure that it was not. Since she had no valid receipt to prove its value, he offered her a casual $100,000 for the painting. Your guess is as good as mine on the outcome. She refused to sell and went on to discover from other galleries in New York that it was indeed genuine and worth in excess of $11 million.

Can you imagine the number of years that the painting lay wasting away in someone's attic or garage before being flung for just $5 in a street market, only to sit behind a smoke-filled truck cabin for years while its various owners all the while lived from hand-to-mouth and laboured in hard jobs.

The revelation to write this book and its intended purpose is to open the eyes of you the reader, to the abundant potential and deposits in you that have been placed there to give you the good life. My prayer for you as you read is that the eyes of your understanding may be enlightened, to know what God has placed already in you for your benefit as you serve Him faithfully.

✺

Chapter 1

The Million Dollar Gem in You

"Every Person has buried deep inside a dazzling, million-dollar gem. We just need to cut away the dirt to find it"---Dr A. J. Twerski

Car boot sales are usually very interesting experiences. Someone opens up their garage or garden shed or loft compartment and brings out those items that may have been left there for months, maybe even years; stuff thought to be no more useful.

You remember that old wine cooler you wanted to throw away; those items of clothing you have outgrown or can no more put on because you have dropped or added some cloth sizes since you bought them. That pair of shoes you never really liked. The old and long abandoned china which you left in the garden shed to save space in your cupboard. The cutlery, that make-up case you once liked so much…. The list is endless. Reluctantly you load them into your car and off you go, saying to yourself, "Let me just hope there will be someone who may have need of these "useless" stuff."

But to your greatest surprise, as you flipped open the boot of your car, you were thronged. "The china is just what I was hoping I'd get", the lady to your left said; and you wonder if she was actually referring to your own china!

Before long, you realize that you need help with the amount of cash in your hands. It still looks too good to be true. You suddenly realize that the very things you had, which you thought did not amount to much, are actually valuable to other people.

There are very many useful self – help books available for any serious person who wishes to improve themselves in whatever field of life. I have benefitted immensely from the insights of many authors who cared enough for the development of others to pen their thoughts.

In **"Unlocking The Harvest Within You",** it is my hope that I can add to the efforts and insights from others towards making you the reader, the very best that God created you to be. This shall be achieved by helping you discover and maximise the vast potentials deposited in you by your Maker.

In Chapter 10, I have written ten practical suggestions which I believe can help the reader to begin the process of unlocking the harvest in them and enjoy God's abundance as was intended for them.

✵

Chapter 2

Your "Garden House"

After reading the painful experience of one of my mentors, who suffered a major health scare after he turned 55, I had to make some very serious decisions about my physical body.

Probably the toughest was the decision to register with my local gym and exercise at least four times each week. (My gym actually recommends 30 minutes of exercising for 5 days of each week. A very tall order for a man who has a hundred and one things screaming for my time each day).

I decided to find a way to enjoy those "agonizing" early days at the gym and I discovered one way was to try and watch the TV screens while my legs and body kept pace with the treadmill. That was how I got into watching a BBC program called *Antiques Road Show*. I do watch TV at home when I have the time, but I am all for News, Movies and Documentaries and the like. No soaps or reality TV at all.

Since I had time on my hands, I did follow this particular episode which featured a lady and her husband, both of whom had raised grown-up children. As a family, they always dreamt of a family holiday to Kenya, East Africa, where the lady was brought up. Her parents had been expatriates there. She was also born there. The trouble was that they were unable to afford such a trip due to their limited resources.

Since returning to the UK decades ago, her number one wish was always to go back with her children even if on a short holiday. She treasured the photographs of the "good old days" in Kenya and would often show them proudly to her children. Those beautiful beaches! The Safari and all! Her children had heard enough about Kenya. The only trouble was that the chances of them seeing it for real was very slim at the time and getting slimmer as the days went by.

The family had been living in their lovely house for many years. The husband was a dentist; and they had acquired so much stuff over the years and, as it is in any typical family house, a lot of the stuff was now "useless".

This was all going to change when an expert in antiques visited.

The man went through the house methodically from one room to the next room. After having gone through the stuff in the first room, the expert stood there dumbfounded and asked her, "Do you have a clue how much money you have in this room?" She answered, "There is no money here".

The expert picked up a particular silver makeup case that was made in the 18th century, which her mother had given to her, but she no longer used. They went to the garden shed and found the dentist cupboard and all kinds of 'useless', abandoned, forgotten and discarded items.

In summary, they went to a bidding session and without even going half way in the process, the dentist cupboard that had been in the garden shed fetched more than £800. Also, an old trunk that the children sat on and the grandchildren had all messed-up, was brought for auction, and it fetched more than £300. The grandmother's silver-plated makeup case fetched £250. There was also a disused birdhouse that the lady's mother had bought for her, when they returned from Kenya. It fetched her £450. The family was shell-shocked.

Is it not the case that sometimes we spend all of our lives chasing those things outside of us, at the expense of the harvest we actually have within us, within our house or within our reach. As human beings, we tend to value what we do not have, more often than what we have.

There's A Million Dollar Gem Buried In Your 'Garden House'.

Everyone has some treasure buried in or around them and that includes you. Let's refer to the story of a certain widow in the Bible:

2 Kings 4:1-2
A certain woman of the wives of the sons of the prophets cried out to Elisha, saying, "Your servant my husband is dead, and you know that your servant feared the Lord. And the creditor is coming to take my two sons to be his slaves." 2 So Elisha said to her, "What shall I do for you? Tell me, what do you have in the house?" And she said, "Your maidservant has nothing in the house but a jar of oil."

For this widow in her trouble, her opinion of what she had in her house was (1) "Nothing" and (2) –"---but a Jar of Oil".

The Message Bible puts her answer to the prophet like this:

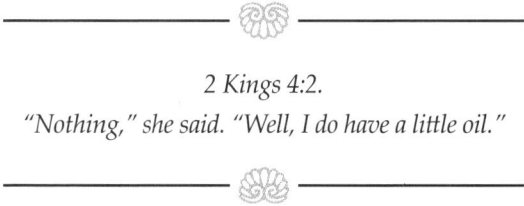

2 Kings 4:2.
"Nothing," she said. "Well, I do have a little oil."

The average human tendency is to minimize and see what we have as 'nothing' or 'little' and while we tend to maximize what we don't have and see them as the being much more important and significant than the former.

As long as that is your point of view, you may never see its value and therefore, may never realize what it was meant, by God, to accomplish in and for your life.

I have discovered that many times, people struggle endlessly seeking such things they believe will improve their situations in life. They labour so hard at getting these things, agonising through one anxious moment after another, while the very answers they sought were right with them all along awaiting discovery and processing.

Until you as an individual will take the time and diligence to explore these long – ignored valuables around you, you are quite likely to continue to struggle endlessly.

*

Chapter 3

Living Involves Challenges

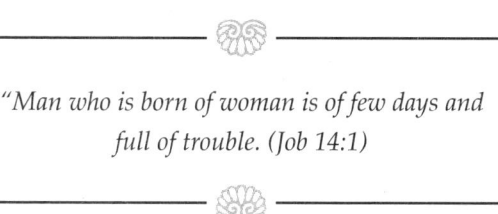

"Man who is born of woman is of few days and full of trouble. (Job 14:1)

Everyone Faces Trouble.

Here, we see the story of a widow in the days of Elisha. Her late husband was one of the prophets who "feared the Lord". A righteous man! Some Bible teachers have speculated that this may have been the prophet Obadiah, who ministered during the reign of King Ahab. I must mention that the Holy Scriptures did not say specifically who he was.

Either way, this woman's husband was righteous and feared The Lord. He served God faithfully during his lifetime.

I often struggle with this paradox: how someone who fears God and serves Him with his life would end up being so challenged financially that he would die leaving a crippling debt, rather than an inheritance, for his wife and sons. This effectively contradicts the provisions of the promises of God to His children and servants.

Yet, it does happen, not only in biblical times but evidently today as well. Every child of God, including those who serve Him in Ministry, must take heed otherwise this very challenge could tarnish our testimonies and question the authenticity of our faith.

While this situation may not be rare in our time, the truth remains that it is not the will of God for His children, especially those who serve Him faithfully like this man did. Remember, God said of the Levites, "I am their portion". This is certainly not God's will for His children, let alone His ministers.

Life sometimes places you on a road that will test you to the limits. If you have ever been on that road, you will agree with me readily. If you have not yet experienced it in your life, be strengthened and encouraged, for sooner or later, you ***will*** walk that road.

God does not intend for you to be defeated or die on that road. He plans only victory for His children. Know that God will sometime, at a certain point in your life, allow you to be brought into a situation where your faith will be tested, not to destroy you but to make you stronger.

If you call God your Father, He will want you to grow in your knowledge and dependence upon Him. Spiritual growth and maturity, is similar to making a decision to build your muscles and keep fit by going to the gym.

The first day you try out twenty kilos and your muscles cry out, you may feel like stopping; but when you see other people walk in, (looking like they were crafted by carpenters; looking so strong and muscular; with no tummy bulge) you wonder how they did it. If you want to look like them, then you have to persevere.

Every believer goes through the testing of their faith. The adversary of your faith, Satan, in particular would like to see you quit half way. But God is with you.

Apostle Paul's Own Experience.

2 Cor 1:8-11
For we do not want you to be ignorant, brethren, of our trouble which came to us in Asia: that we were burdened beyond measure, above strength, so that we despaired even of life. 9 Yes, we had the sentence of death in ourselves, that we should not trust in ourselves but in God who raises the dead, 10 who delivered us from so great a death, and does deliver us; in whom we trust that He will still deliver us, 11 you also helping together in prayer for us, that thanks may be given by many persons on our behalf for the gift granted to us through many.

In Asia, Paul was stoned more than once. In Acts chapter 19, while ministering in the city of Ephesus, the silversmith, Demetrius, ignited uproar against Paul and his team; from city to city, they sought to kill him. He was stoned many times. They would leave him at the seaside, with a heap of stones over him, and he would just get up, dust himself and go into the next city to preach. Paul suffered so much such that in verse 9 above, Paul wrote "*Yes, we had the sentence of death in ourselves....*"

Apostle Paul wants you to know that you will go through trying situations that will test your faith, and pressures of life that will bring you to a seeming dead end. Have you ever been there? Just when you thought the miracle was about to break through, the delay becomes even longer.

I call it "**delay by design**". Apostle Paul said he had given up all hope that he should stay alive. He actually believed that the sentence of death had been passed on him and his team. He had probably accepted that it was the will of God for him to die, but he survived it. That is why he could write to us telling us that this happened so that we will not rely on ourselves, but on the True and Living God.

What does it mean to depend on yourself? It means, in a very basic sense, to depend on your wisdom, intellect, connections, husband, wife or bank account balance, strength, skills, etc., for your wellbeing and survival. If your joy is based on what you have, you are in serious trouble. This is why some people kill others, and some end their own lives, because their joy was dependent on what they had.

> Verses 9b and 10 says, "..........*that we should not trust in ourselves but in God who raises the dead, who delivered us from so great a death, and does deliver us; in whom we trust that He will still deliver us,*

Even if the situation appears dead, God can bring it back to life for you. God is dependable. The bank may fail, the company may close, your job may end but God cannot fail nor can He lie. Paul lived through it to tell us that we can depend upon God. I am confident that if God was able to do it before in Paul's life, he definitely is able to do it again in your life.

Get ready for a different perspective on the situation! There is a powerful revelation coming to you in a moment and it will transform your life completely and open your eyes to the goodness of God in your life.

It Is Not The Challenge You Face But Your Revelation

The Prophet Elisha, responded to the widow with a question rather than an offer of a 'very special prophetic prayer' for her – **"What do you have in your house?"**

In the life of every believer in Christ, there is a deposit, a potential or measure of grace that God has placed in his or her life for times of trouble. The challenge is discovering and deploying this potential. This is primarily, what this book seeks to unravel.

When faced with trouble, the first response God expects of you is to find out what resources and potentials are at your disposal. If you have a healthy knowledge of God, and of whom He is, you will understand that He will never allow His own to go into battle without equipping them effectively for it.

The political argument in Britain today (as at the time of this writing), is whether our armed forces in Afghanistan have enough and adequate equipment to do the job our government has asked of them. As a nation, no matter how much military equipment the government offers the soldiers, there will always be the need for more. The British chief of general staff confirmed this when he said that you can never have enough equipment.

However, did you know that it is not so with God? Before you go into any battle, He has already equipped you for that fight, before any enemy comes against your life, or appears on the scene, The Lord would have already made provision for situation.

- *The Lord God has unlimited and inexhaustible amount of resources.*
- *He also has Perfect knowledge of the enemy's capability and strategies,*
- *God also has complete control of the outcome of any fight you will ever be involved in the course of your walk with Him.*

In this book, my aim is to challenge us, the believers, so as to open our eyes to the things that we think are nothing – things we ignore because we want to see the "bigger miracle", without looking at the 'little' things that God has provided for us, which actually are the small dots, which when connected purposefully, reveal the 'big miracles' we are expecting.

✷

Chapter 4

Essential Reminders.

I have grown to realize that the size of a man's fight is nearly not as important as the amount of relevant information available to him while in the fight. That may, in a sense, account for why nations spend vast amounts of money in intelligence gathering in order to be prepared for any eventualities that may arise at any time.

We live in very uncertain times. For the serious believer in Christ, the present day 'virus' of quick-fix Christianity must be intentionally replaced by a sincere desire to investigate God's provisions for us as is contained in His word and a readiness to do what it says while patiently waiting for its manifestation. To help in this journey, there are a few very important reminders I want to bring to my readers' attention.

You Are Not Meant To Fight Alone.

There are people strategically placed in your life and around you specifically to help you in whatever situation you may find yourself. Your capacity to recognize them and work accordingly with them is vital.

The prophet Elisha said to the widow, 'go to **your neighbours** and borrow not a few vessels.' Do you realize that the widow's neighbours played a vital role in her miracle?

In *1 Samuel 30,* David had lost his home, his two wives, children and everything he had. The people with him cried so much that the Bible says there was no strength left in them to cry, and they even thought of stoning David. But the Bible says David encouraged himself in the Lord his God. He prayed to God, "should I pursue this people, will I overtake them and will I recover everything I've lost?" God said, "Pursue them, and you will surely overtake them and without fail, you will recover everything you've lost."

God gave David this promise but how would David know where they were? What was the connection to its fulfilment? It was through a slave Egyptian who was sick, and was left behind by his master to die.

David could have seen him and said, "This must be one of them, kill him"; but rather, they brought the Egyptian to David and he fed him.

For every Abraham, there will always be an Eliezer of Damascus. For every Moses, God will assign a Joshua, Aaron and Hur. For every Saul, there will always be an Abner, the son of Ner and for every David, God will always assign a Joab. For Jesus' burial place, God will always raise up a Joseph from Arimathea.

Correctly identifying and harnessing the relationships God places in your life will not only make your journey easier but will also provide for you those things you do not possess but which others do.

I shall develop this principle a little further in chapter 5.

Prayer Opens Doors

The earnest (heartfelt, continued) prayer of a righteous man makes tremendous power available [dynamic in its working]. James 5:16b (Amp)

The widow came to Elisha because she had a need and it was a real need. A need that was so bad that her two sons were going into slavery. When you are really in trouble, what is your first reaction? The majority will say, "Pray", but my question is, what do you call prayer? How do you pray in such times if at all you can pray? Let me tell you, if you really are in a storm, the default mode would be more likely self-pity than prayer.

However, we must learn from this woman. The Bible says she went to Elisha during her very difficult time. He was the minister of God, the prophet to the nation, the judge of the nation at the time, so it was like going to God. At the time, the Holy Spirit was not yet given to all men. But she knew that Elisha was able to hear from God.

She knew that by going to Elisha, he would hear from God and that God would answer his prayers. Prayer is the most important key.

The next question would be, what kind of prayer do you pray when you are in trouble? What is your attitude when you are in trouble? Even when you make up your mind to pray, what is the attitude behind that prayer? Many find themselves complaining rather than pray in faith. Don't be too hard on yourself because not everybody can pray by faith during times of trouble. In real trouble, you are more likely to complain and you can imagine God listening and saying, "Where is your faith?"

But without faith it is impossible to please him: for he that comes to God must believe that he is, and that he is a rewarder of those who diligently seek Him. **Hebrews 11:6**

In the Amplified Version, it says

Without faith, it is impossible to please and be satisfactory with God. For whoever would come near to God would necessarily believe that God exists, and that He is a rewarder of those who earnestly and diligently seek him

---

God does not reward casual visitors who just want to receive from His hands. I am aware that many people preach that you should just come and God will give you a miracle, no matter how you live but

I wonder how many of those miracles produce the results that glorify God in heaven. God rewards those that take time to relate to Him.

Prayer is not just coming to God and wanting Him to conform to and bring Himself into your own plans. It is about you coming and saying, "Lord, I am ready to align with your own plans for my life."

Do you realize God's plans are bigger, better, more inclusive than yours? It goes beyond what we could ever imagine or think; so when you come to Him and say, "Lord, help me fit into your plans", what happens is He begins to unfold to you the depths of His purpose for your life.

While this is not a book on prayer, I must nonetheless remind you that prayer is irreplaceable in your life as a Christian. It does not matter whether you like to pray or not. It does not even matter whether you "know" how to pray or not. The important thing during life challenges is that you must make the time to talk to God about His Covenant Promises. Remind Him of His infallible Word and wait for His answers in return. Prayer works!

YOUR WANT vs. YOUR NEED.

Phil 4:19
*And my God shall supply all your **need**
according to His riches in glory
by Christ Jesus.*

God only promises to supply the things you need and not the things you want. Think for a moment about that.

The widow came to Elisha and told him exactly what she needed. Elisha asked her two questions in response, "What do you have in your house and what do you want me to do for you?" Sometimes, we get into situations and we are unable to define in prayers to God, what we *need*. Rather, we go to God with what we *want*.

Success or failure in life, in a very real sense, is driven largely by the individual's ability to distinguish between what they 'want' and what they 'need'. God's Word guarantees that He will faithfully supply "all your need according to His riches in glory by Jesus Christ", not our wants. (Philippians 4:19).

You will enjoy more of God's peace in any area of your life only to the degree that you are able to resolve the difference between what you want and what you need at any particular time in that area of your life.

When you go to God in prayers asking for a miracle generally, as many Christians do, the question would be: "What specific miracle are you asking for?" King Solomon in first Kings offered a thousand bulls to God and God appeared to him at night saying to him, "What do you want me to do for you?"

Blind Bartimaeus cried out, "Jesus, the son of David, have mercy on me". The crowd tried to shut him down, insinuating that Jesus did not come for someone like him. The more they told him to keep quiet, the louder he cried. If you read the two accounts of this story, this man cried when Jesus was coming into town.

He kept crying until Jesus finished his business and was leaving town. Even though Jesus didn't answer him when he was coming into the town, Bartimaeus made up his mind that Jesus would answer his prayer before He left town. When the people told him to stop, Bartimaeus cried out the more, until he attracted the attention of Jesus. Jesus stopped and turned towards him. The first thing Jesus asked him when they brought Mr. Bartimaeus to him was, "What do you want me to do for you?"

Your ability to clearly articulate what you need from God is a primary key in effective praying. You have to know what you need, not necessarily what you want. You have to draw the line between needs and wants. God is interested in what you need.

Every person in any form of trouble or challenge should be able to answer this question, "What do I need in this situation?" The correct answer to that question will open the door out for you. You can not just say, "God, give me a miracle". What kind of miracle do you want? In the situation that you find yourself, you have to identify your need.

There is a difference between asking God to put food on the table every day and asking Him for the means to feed yourself, your family and be a blessing to other people. There is a difference between, "I want a job" – any non – secure job, for example – and "Lord, I need a job that will settle me, or a business that will establish me".

Go for what you need and not what you want.

Your Identity In Christ

I am completely overwhelmed by the knowledge of the richness of the Biblical identity of the believer in Christ. It transcends the limitations of the natural birth or educational and career attainments because we are sons and joint-heirs with Christ in the kingdom. This is phenomenal. It is a radical revelation.

John 1:11-13
He came to His own, and His own did not receive Him. 12 But as many as received Him, to them He gave the right to become children of God, to those who believe in His name: 13 who were born, not of blood, nor of the will of the flesh, nor of the will of man, but of God.

When a person yields their heart to the Lord and surrenders to His Lordship, they instantly receive the God-given authority, power, privilege or right to become what they could never have been on their own – the sons and daughters of God. This is a very important and a powerful reminder that we are no longer strangers in the courts of heaven but joint heirs with The Lord Jesus.

In John 5:16–18 and John 10:30-34, the Bible says that as Jesus did these miracles, people took up stones to kill Him and He said to them, "for which of the miracles are you trying to kill me?" They said to him, "we are not killing you for the good things you have done, but because you, being a man say you are the son of God, thereby making yourself equal with God; claiming equality with divinity by saying you are the Son of God." Now, that gives us information that it is not ordinary when we say we are children of God. That should make everyone know that they are not ordinary persons anymore.

Have you ever considered the rights and privileges of a son or daughter in their Father's house? The prodigal son's Father told the older son, "Son, everything I have is yours".

So the question, 'Who are you?' has been answered. You are a child of God and have the covenant right to everything your Father has.

Don't Ignore What Is Yours!

This is what this book is really about. I once read the story of a couple who bought a property. One day, as the family increased in number, the man decided to clear out the attic in order to make more storage room available. While on it, he stumbled upon a treasure trove of cash.

Obviously, it had been left there by a previous owner or tenant. It may have been there several decades before he bought the property. Just imagine that. The question is, "What is in your house?" What gift has God placed in you? What is it that you do effortlessly? What is 'your thing'? What is it you simply enjoy doing? When you discover it, you go for it with everything you have, as the Scripture teaches in:

Matthew 13:44,
"Again, the kingdom of heaven is like treasure hidden in a field, which a man found and hid; and for joy over it he goes and sells all that he has and buys that field.

The first answer the widow gave to that question is, "Nothing". Maybe she expected Elisha to pray for her or give her from the Ministry treasury, but Elisha turned around and asked her, "What do you have in the house?"

Now, let's look at it in some more detail: the widow had a jar of oil, so, at least, she knew she had something; she knew what she had even though she called it "nothing".

Your jar of oil could be anything unique to you. We will begin to explore the possibilities of what that jar of oil could be. Did you notice that while that jar of oil had been with her, it meant nothing to her? It was probably there before her husband died. They would most probably have bought much more than the 'little' that was leftover.

Creditors would, as a matter of standard practice, send you demand notice after demand notice, when the bill is overdue for settlement. Then they will most likely send notices reminding the debtor of their plans to take legal actions. It is when this fails to yield results that they would apply to the courts of law to visit the debtor and take whatever valuable items they can find. In those days, the probable action would have been to take her sons to work as slaves for the creditors, to work without pay until the debt would have been cleared by their labour.

Imagine that all the while these letters were coming from the creditors; the jar of oil had been in the widow's house. The creditors may have probably set a date to visit the widow; meanwhile the jar of oil was in the house. She must have spent sleepless nights crying and maybe begging everyone she could find for help while the jar of oil was still in her house. I hope you are seeing what I am driving at here?

This revelation will not benefit you if at the end of reading this book you fail to do whatever is necessary in order to discover what you have been given by God that is uniquely yours. God has equipped you for whatever you are facing right now and has provided for the journey to wherever you are going in your life. It is my prayer that God will open the eyes of your understanding today in Jesus Name.

The widow said to Elisha, "I have nothing save a little jar of oil." To her, it was insignificant. It was "nothing". It could not possibly be the miracle she needed, or could it?

Ask Yourself The Right Questions.

Voltaire, an 18th Century thinker said, "Judge a man by the questions he asks rather than by the answers he gives." I read this recently and it made a lot of sense to me. A lot of us are not good at asking ourselves important questions, and until you're able to ask yourself serious questions, you may not really discover who you are and what you have.

The key to discovering what you have in your house lies in your ability to ask yourself serious questions and in beginning the process of exploring the relevant answers. If you fail to question yourself, you are likely to repeat the mistakes you have made before, and continue to live your life the same old way.

You should be able to ask yourself, "Who am I in Christ?" You might be going through challenges, or you desire a change in life; regarding where you are at this point, and where you want to be in the near future. You should be able to answer yourself that question intentionally and say to yourself, "I am a child of God". Then, ask yourself again, if you were God and you had a son or sons, you had all the riches and you said, "I love this child", would you want to see him suffer?

Could it be that God has another plan, a better plan for you? The moment you start to ask yourself serious questions, you will discover what you probably have never discovered about yourself.

You need to be able to ask yourself the question, "What do I really need?" "Where do I really start from?" "What do I have?" "What are my strengths"? "What are my skills"? "What can I do without much stress"? "How can I turn that into what other people need"? "What can I start doing without a lot of money"? "What do I have, which I have long neglected or ignored?"

Dr. Mike Murdock, a man of God says "the things you despise, you lose; the things you appreciate or value, you attract". Let's break it down: from my experience as a pastor, I've seen people sell themselves short because of the value they placed on themselves. When they appear on the scene, they prize themselves less than what they could have been valued for, because they sell themselves as good-for-nothings.

You should learn to place an appropriate or reasonable value on yourself. I am not talking about being arrogant, I am talking about actually sincerely assessing who you really are and what you are worth and asking yourself the question, "Who am I?"

When you have the correct value of yourself or your worth, no one can succeed in telling you otherwise.

Remember, No one will ever value you beyond the price you place on yourself!

I have met people who are very qualified academically but they still define themselves by their past, where they have been, what they have gone through, what they have suffered, the rejection they suffered, or what a friend said about them. What about all the value that God has invested in them?

When they look in the mirror every morning, all they see or think of themselves is that man that rejected them or their childhood sweetheart that they thought they were going to marry and he or she moved on with someone else.

You cannot define yourself by what you've gone through or what people say of you. You cannot control other people's opinion of you, but what you think of yourself is what is important. It is often said and truly so that "what lies behind you is nearly not as important as what lies ahead of you"

> Even our Lord Jesus needed to be certain of who his chosen disciples thought He was. He asked His disciples,*Who do men say I, The Son of Man, am?"* They answered Him *"Some say John the Baptist, some Elijah, and others Jeremiah or one of the prophets."*
> (Matt 16:13, 14).

Jesus replied them saying, *"But Who do you say that I am?"* In other words, it does not matter so much what other people see or say of me but it matters who you say I am.

Observe the silence of the eleven disciples. How loud! We tend to be more readily acquainted with other people's opinion of things and even of us. What do you say of you! Of the twelve, only one had a revelation of who Jesus is. Peter, said, *"You are the Christ, the Son of the living God"*.

When you lack the proper revelation of who you are, you will only walk around with the revelation or opinion of other people for you. The Bible says you are fearfully and wonderfully made. You are not defined by what you do not have or possess.

Train Yourself To Walk Away From Your Natural Inclination

The natural human inclination, the default mode of most unregenerate minds, is to dwell on what they do not possess. Jesus taught His disciples a major lesson on this:

Mark 8:13-16.

And he left them, and entering into the ship again departed to the other side. Now the disciples had forgotten to take bread, neither had they in the ship with them more than one loaf. And he charged them, saying, Take heed, beware of the leaven of the Pharisees, and of the leaven of Herod. And they reasoned among themselves, saying, It is because we have no bread

Observe the "reasoning" of the men here. Their minds automatically went to what they did not have, even though the Lord was speaking of something completely different here.

Is that not the state of the average or undeveloped human mind? The moment a situation arises in your life, the first thing that comes to your mind is what you do not have. My intention in writing this book is to help highlight to you what you do have and to focus on developing it no matter how insignificant it may appear at the moment.

Mark 8:17-21

But Jesus, being aware of it, said to them, "Why do you reason because you have no bread? Do you not yet perceive nor understand? Is your heart still hardened? 18 Having eyes, do you not see? And having ears, do you not hear? And do you not remember? 19 When I broke the five loaves for the five thousand, how many baskets full of fragments did you take up?" They said to Him, "Twelve." 20 "Also, when I broke the seven for the four thousand, how many large baskets full of fragments did you take up?" And they said, "Seven." 21 So He said to them, ***"How is it you do not understand?"***

Anytime a need arises in the unregenerate mind or the natural human mind, it naturally goes to what we don't have. This type of thinking can only produce fear, doubt, unbelief and panic in your heart. Immediately a need arises, like the widow we read about, the first thing that comes to the mind is, "I don't have the money", "I can't do it", "I don't have the skills", "I have no man to help me", "I am not educated",…..

Jesus spoke to the disciples to beware of the leaven of the Pharisees and of Herod, and their minds went immediately to not having bread. Jesus asked, "What is wrong with you people"? Is your mind still hardened or is it not about time you renewed your mind and started to think differently? Like Paul said in 2 Corinthians 8, the reason this happened is that we could rely, not on ourselves but, on God because He has saved us before and will always save us.

Can you imagine your mind being so positioned that the moment a situation arises, your first reaction is: "God has seen me through this before, He will me see me through it yet again".

Jesus is saying that the natural mind will go to: "I do not have"; but what I really want you to do, where you should be, the place of power, dominion and victory, where you are in control, if you want to be victorious is – to be able to react firstly, not with respect to what you do not have, but with the fact that you remember that when such and such happened, He did it for you.

He brought you through it before; He will bring you through it yet again. Do you realize what leverage this will give you in life? Famous American coach, the late John Wooden said: "Don't let what you do not have, stop you from doing what you can *and should* do"!

Remember, God Is Ever Faithful

Always remind yourself that God is faithful. Fill your heart with that revelation daily. Know that He can never abandon you no matter what happens. Naturally, your heart will be troubled but there is something beyond the struggle.

It is only human to feel some fear when trouble comes, but don't stop there. It must never dominate your mind and thoughts. Develop and sustain a dominant, positive, faith-on–the-word thought pattern in your mind.

Philippians 1:6 (AMP)

And I am convinced and sure of this very thing, that He Who began a good work in you will continue until the day of Jesus Christ [right up to the time of His return], developing [that good work] and perfecting and bringing it to full completion in you.

This means The Lord God has no intention of giving up on you midway. He is developing that good work, perfecting it and bringing it to full completion in you. Jesus wants us, who are believers in Him, to set our minds, whenever trouble comes, to remember that you are not of yourselves, you belong to Him, and He who started this work is still at work; and even though the situation may appear difficult now, be sure He has saved you before and He will save you yet again.

Encourage yourself by saying to yourself, "God is at work in my life, I'm not about to give up before my change comes". It means He started it, He is at work, you are not alone, and He will see you through. With such a mindset, you may be afraid but will never be fearful in the face of difficulties.

Romans 8:28 says:

And we know that all things work together for good to them that love God, to them who are the called according to his purpose.
Romans 8:28

Things will turn out well, because of you.

Has God delivered you from a dire financial challenge before, or healed your physical body? Has He ever delivered you from trouble or shame that threatened to engulf you? Remind yourself that if God did that, you have no business losing your peace. The God, who did that for you in the past, promises never to sleep or slumber. He will do it again for you. The victory is in you.

✳

Chapter 5

Unleash Your Faith.

2 Cor 5:7 (NIV)
"We live by faith, not by sight".

What do you have in your house? Your response, before you started reading this book may have been "I have nothing". Think about the lady in the TV program I referred above, who kept telling her children, year-in, year-out, "Your dad and I cannot afford a holiday to Kenya"; meanwhile, all around them, were stuff that she could have traded to those who needed them.

As long as you keep placing zero value on what you have, your skills, creativity, wisdom, eloquence, artistry, design ability or whatever the Almighty God has deposited in you, it will not bless your life. But the day you awake to the potentials in it, and declare the prophetic word of God, the Word that created the Heavens and the Earth over it, it will begin to flow out and fill every empty jar in your life.

What do you have in your house?

The widow's response was, 'I have nothing.' Thank God she did not stop there. This is exactly where I am trying to get you to. Much of what you need for your life, for where you are at in life, whether in your relationships, career, finances, or even for your Christian faith, has already been supplied.

She said to him, "I have nothing; all I have is a jar of oil." Can you see the size of that jar from her answer? It may have been small, insignificant and good for nothing. That was not what she came to hear. She didn't come to tell him about the things she had in her house- valueless things. In fact, to her, they were junk.

I have good news for you: as you read on, the Spirit of God will help you to reverse your focus, so that rather than look for your dream harvest outside, you can begin from what you have on the inside. What you are searching for outside is actually in your house.

Faith Believes The Impossible And Sees The Invisible.

We have been looking at how Elisha met the needs of the widow woman, as well as the wisdom that surrounded his approach to her challenges and her troubles. He opened her eyes and drew her attention to what God had already provided for her, which according to God's plan, was actually the trigger for her miracle or harvest.

We've looked at Mark 8; where Jesus, upon feeding the people came into the boat with His disciples and said to them, "Beware of the leaven of the Pharisees……" The Bible says they began to reason within themselves saying, "It is because we have no bread" and Jesus said to them, "Why do you reason that you have no bread?" I want you to try and get this picture very clearly in your spirit, because it's so vital. This is a very powerful revelation for you.

At the beginning of Mark 8, Jesus fed the 4,000.

Mark 8:13-16

And he left them, and entering into the ship again departed to the other side. Now the disciples had forgotten to take bread, neither had they in the ship with them more than one loaf. And he charged them, saying, Take heed, beware of the leaven of the Pharisees, and of the leaven of Herod. And they reasoned among themselves, saying, It is because we have no bread.

Immediately, their minds went into the fact that they had no bread and that gives us some insight into how the human mind functions; it gives us an understanding of the natural inclinations and proclivities of the natural mind.

Every time a situation arises that is challenging, the human mind, is naturally inclined, in its unregenerate state, to first see what you do not have and what that does is put fear in your heart. Fear depletes your strength; it makes you fail in your mind even before the situation comes up for mention. Jesus just said, "Beware of the leaven of the Pharisees', and the Bible says they reasoned in their minds meaning, their minds naturally, went by default, into the 'I-do-not-have…' mode.

The woman had a debt to pay and she went to the man of God without even first of all, appreciating what she had in her home. As far as she was concerned, she had nothing and was in debt. Her natural mind could never tell her that maybe there is something she had that could get her out of debt. Her natural mind just went into where it is supposed to go by default, "I don't have, I need help."

It will take a divine revelation for you to see the invisible. It is my prayer for you today that the eyes of your spirit be opened this moment by the Spirit of God, that from this hour, you may begin to see those 'things' which God has already provided for and are in and with you. Your natural mind is not the way God created it to be, it has been corrupted by the fall of man and weakened in its ability to function the way it was created to function.

Hear what The Lord said to the disciples;

Mark 8:17
But Jesus, being aware of it, said to them, "Why do you reason because you have no bread? Do you not yet perceive nor understand? Is your heart still hardened?

In other words, why does your mind go directly unto what you do not have? Often, your thoughts are, "I am going through this because of the fact that I don't have this…."

For you to stand out from the crowd, for you to excel where others are failing, you will have to train your mind to move from the default tendency into where Jesus wants it to be. When situations arise and your mind says, "You can't afford it, you can't do it", let the Spirit of God that is inside you remind you that you can do it, that you have what it takes.

A lady once testified in church of trying to complete her course work online but the computer said to her "command not possible to execute"; but she said, "Jesus you can handle it", and it was done. That's the kind of mindset I'm talking about.

Mark 8:18-21

Having eyes, do you not see? And having ears, do you not hear? And do you not remember? 19 When I broke the five loaves for the five thousand, how many baskets full of fragments did you take up?" They said to Him, "Twelve." 20 "Also, when I broke the seven for the four thousand, how many large baskets full of fragments did you take up?" And they said, "Seven." 21 So He said to them, "How is it you do not understand?"

Your ability to see beyond the obvious is vital in transiting from your present location to your destiny. Beyond the obvious lies 'your own Promised Land'. Seeing the invisible comes with discernment and that is a gift from The Holy Spirit. Consider Joshua on the threshold of destiny.

> *Josh 6:1-2*
> *Now Jericho was securely shut up because of the children of Israel; none went out, and none came in. 2 And the Lord said to Joshua: "See! I have given Jericho into your hand, its king, and the mighty men of valour.*

The verse paints the picture of a closed case. Zero chance here Josh! Simply put, there is no way in for you and your people, Joshua. Joshua had a choice at this juncture to believe the obvious and accept it as the logical reality. He could also accept the invisible reality as spoken by the Almighty God in verse two. Notice that God commands Joshua to first of all "See". Hallelujah!

Beloved, we are called to see beyond the natural and the obvious. You must see the reality that is invisible by the power of the spirit of faith. You cannot hit any target that you do not see. Train yourself to see what God says exists for you. That is the challenge of faith in Hebrews 11 verse 1.

Unleash Your Faith.

It is also the call to partake in the Divine Nature as Apostle Peter so powerfully puts it in

---

2 Peter 1:2-4;

Grace and peace be multiplied to you in the knowledge of God and of Jesus our Lord, 3 as His divine power has given to us all things that pertain to life and godliness, through the knowledge of Him who called us by glory and virtue, 4 by which have been given to us exceedingly great and precious promises, that through these you may be partakers of the divine nature, having escaped the corruption that is in the world through lust.

God's divine power has given to every one of us everything we will ever need for this life. By ascending through the knowledge of Jesus, we possess, through faith, the manifestation of these exceedingly great and precious promises. This is how we were created to operate on the earth.

The Limitless Realm

Elisha said to the widow in 2 Kings 4:3
Then he said, "Go, borrow vessels from everywhere, from all your neighbours — empty vessels; do not gather just a few.

The Bible says she and her sons went to their neighbourhood and collected as many vessels as they could; she locked the door behind her and filled all the vessels. Think about it, all she had was a jar of oil. The vessels referred to here are large containers, perhaps ten or twenty litre containers, and all she had was a little jar, maybe like what you buy from the shop, just enough to cook a meal or two. Yet every container she could get was filled. As long as there were empty containers, the oil kept on flowing and filling them up.

The only time the oil ceased was when she had no more empty containers to fill. Think about that for a moment.

Allow me to digress here and intimate you with what I call '**the unceasing grace of God**.' God's grace will continue to be sufficient for you as long as the hunger and desire remains in you. The more you desire to see the manifestation of God's power, the more He will show up for you. That is why there is no room for quitters in the Kingdom.

You just cannot afford to quit no matter how dire the situation may appear to be. One of the meanings we are taught of the name of God, El-Shaddai, is that He is the God that is more than enough. In other words, He is simply inexhaustible. How many empty vessels do you have? Get ready! God is ready to fill them all up for you.

The Lord Jesus gave the church what I would dare call 'a blank cheque' in

---

Mark 11:24

Therefore I say to you, whatever things you ask when you pray, believe that you receive them, and you will have them.

As long as you can believe that God is not only able but willing as well to do it for you, Jesus said you can ask whatever things you need. Of course they must be in line with God's Word. Limitless indeed!

Shut That Door Behind You!

She went and shut the door behind her. Have you ever asked yourself what the significance of shutting that door is? Jesus said, "When you pray, go into your closet and shut the door behind you…" That is the same application. What does that mean? It means you should shut out the noise. Do you know what noise is? Noise is sounds or voices that don't make sense. According to the free online dictionary, Wikipedia, the word **noise** means 'any unwanted sound'. Noise is 'random unwanted perturbation to a wanted signal'.

Do you know what those voices are? Do you know that you can actually shut the door of your room and yet still be hearing noise? The noise I am referring to, is not the booming loudspeaker in the young man's car downstairs? I'm talking about the noise in your heart, the voices that are screaming at you and saying, 'This is foolish! How could you attempt to pour from this little jar into a 20 litre vessel?" "What is wrong with you?" "Have you lost your mind?" "If you were realistic, if you were rational, if you were logical, you would know that there is no way you would pour from the jar into all these vessels". That's noise. Shut them all out.

'God's talk' or instructions, sometimes do not agree much with human reasoning. I suggest you find a convenient place, where you can be alone with God. Do your best to calm your spirit down. Spend as much time as is necessary to meditate on the promise of God that relates to where you are or what is in your heart. Intentionally cast away every negative thought, imagination, experiences of past failures, or any thought that is capable of introducing doubt or unbelief in your heart. Confess the promise repeatedly to yourself. Declare that you believe what it says. Tell The Lord to bring it to pass in your life as He has promised.

※

Chapter 6

Authentic Relationships Are Important

The Borrowed Vessels!

Let us look more closely at the vessels she borrowed. It is possible to look at the miracle and forget the powerful details surrounding the miracle itself. What if she had no good relationship with the neighbours? She would have had the jar of oil but no vessels. The man of God had spoken, "Go borrow vessels from your neighbours and pour out."

But what if she had no friendly neighbours to borrow from? Think about it. It is not just about having the jar of oil that is the key to your miracle, connecting with your community properly is even more important. In Christendom, we have the ungodly, unscriptural tendency to separate from the world. That is not in line with the teachings of Christ.

He never told us to separate ourselves completely from the world, He only told us not to be like the world. Elisha did not specify that she should borrow from the other sons of the prophets in the monastery. What if they did not have what she wanted? He said, "Go, borrow from your neighbours". The King James Version actually used the word "abroad"; which the NKJV translates "everywhere"

Notice the Prophet specified "from all your neighbours", not from neighbours you like or who like you, but, from **all** of your neighbours. You will need the people around you!

King David Needed An Egyptian Slave.

In 1 Samuel 30, the Amalekites had attacked Ziklag and taken David's two wives, and all his children as captives. They took everything David and his 'band of brothers' possessed. The Bible says the people that were with him wept so much that they had no more strength to weep and on top of that, they thought of stoning David. He prayed, "God, should I pursue these people, shall I overtake them?" God said, "Go after them, pursue them for you shall surely overtake them and without fail, you shall recover all."

David had received the confirmation from God he was asking for. The next question would then be where to find them? The raiders might have gone toward the North, South, East or the West. Should David head in the wrong direction, he will not only waste valuable time; but risk not finding this troop and his family and possessions altogether.

There was of course the added risk of taking on the wrong band of invaders. David's army could be depleted, more time wasted even before he engaged the real enemy. The odds were stacked against David. He needed the right direction, some reliable intelligence, a dependable connection.

The Bible says David saw a sick Egyptian slave who was left behind by his master to die in the desert. For many days, he had not eaten. David had enough trouble on his hands already. The men around him were even thinking of stoning him, his best of friends. Imagine that! David's two wives and children, and everything else he had were gone. The uniqueness of King David's life was such that even in the moment of his deepest despair, he never lost his common touch.

I am concerned for Christians, who are so big today, that they can not see the 'common' people around them, who may actually be the key to their needs. They are so 'holy', they can't relate to other human beings, especially non-Christians. Others are so overwhelmed by their own individual challenges, that they have no time for the needs of other people around them which they could so easily solve, should they ever bother to help.

Your blessings and progress are inter-connected with the people God has placed on your path. You need them. Begin to recognize, appreciate, honour and celebrate them. See how you can be of help and serve them even in little ways. Who knows?

The Bible says, when they brought the Egyptian to David in his state of need, David fed him, clothed him and gave him water to drink.

> ***1 Sam 30:13-15***
>
> *Then David said to him, "To whom do you belong, and where are you from?" And he said, "I am a young man from Egypt, servant of an Amalekite; and my master left me behind, because three days ago I fell sick. 14 We made an invasion of the southern area of the Cherethites, in the territory which belongs to Judah, and of the southern area of Caleb; and we burned Ziklag with fire." 15 And David said to him, "Can you take me down to this troop?" So he said, "Swear to me by God that you will neither kill me nor deliver me into the hands of my master, and I will take you down to this troop."*

I suggest you take a second and better look at your relationship with your immediate community. Your brothers and sisters, your colleagues at work, in the church or your family and the people around you in general.

Your Relationships Must Be Authentic.

Beware of trying to form relationships with people for ulterior or selfish motives. I am convinced that the more authentic our relationships with the people around us are, the more they will take us and our faith much more seriously.

When you try to build a relationship with people for the wrong reasons, they will know! The depth of your commitment in any relationship, what you are willing to sacrifice or otherwise for the relationship, will always speak louder than your words.

The need to make a conscious decision to represent and showcase the love of Christ in our relationships cannot be over emphasized. This is particularly important when you know that others may be very closely connected with God's plans and purposes for your life.

Insecurity Kills Relationships.

This is something to avoid if you wish to build authentic connections with others. Unnecessary suspicions, allowing fear to dominate your thoughts and life will certainly drive you into presenting different personalities at different times and maybe to different people. How do the people around you see you? Are they able to willingly and without any pressure release their 'vessels' to you and your children? If you are closed up and locked in, they may not.

Let us assume, for instance, that the widow in 2 Kings 4 was an insecure, proud and arrogant woman, and all the neighbours knew that of her. Imagine her sons showing up at their doorstep and saying, "our mom would like to borrow your vessels to pour her oil into them." I will leave you to guess what the likely response of her neighbours would have been.

Lessons From Ants

Proverbs 30:24-28, says,
There be four things which are little upon the earth, but they are exceeding wise: The ants are a people not strong, yet they prepare their meat in the summer; The conies are but a feeble folk, yet make they their houses in the rocks; The locusts have no king, yet go they forth all of them by bands; The spider taketh hold with her hands, and is in kings' palaces.

You will observe something common to these four little creatures: they are small on the earth but they are wise. As a matter of fact, in Proverbs 6:6, the Bible says, *"Go to the Ant, you sluggard! Consider her ways, and be wise."* He commands the sluggard to go to the ants and learn how to live. The question is, who are the ants? If the scripture defines the ants as wise, one of the things that make ants successful is teamwork. Do you realize that ants go together? Let me give you some facts about ants, this will bless you as it has really blessed me.

a. They are small in size but it is estimated that the combined weight of all the ants in the world, is more than all the combined weight of human beings.

b. Ants are known to successfully move pieces of food which are sometimes 10 – 20 times their body mass.

c. The Bible calls them wise;

d. Some anthills could be as tall as a building and some are equally as massive as half the size of an average room? How would a little ant build such a structure? It is through teamwork.

e. It has been suggested that an ant's brain may have the same processing power as an Apple Mac 2 computer.

f. Another thing about ants is they are never hungry out of season because they always provide their food when they need it.

The Bible says we should learn wisdom from them. One strand of wisdom I want us to learn from ants is the respect they have for one another. Each ant believes in the other; each ant subscribes to the strength of the other; they complement one another in their efforts at getting things done. That is wisdom. Two is better than one!

If you are serious about starting the process of harvesting from within, harvesting the potentials that are within you, bringing out the best from what you have, then, a great starting point would be to invest just a little more in your relationships with the people around you. It's time to believe more in them. It's time for you to stop seeing yourself as better than they are. No one person is better than or inferior to any other in the sight of God. We are all in dire need of God's grace to be acceptable to Him.

> Eccl 4:8-12 (NKJV)
>
> *There is one alone, without companion: He has neither son nor brother. Yet there is no end to all his labors, Nor is his eye satisfied with riches. But he never asks, "For whom do I toil and deprive myself of good?" This also is vanity and a grave misfortune. 9 Two are better than one, Because they have a good reward for their labor. 10 For if they fall, one will lift up his companion. But woe to him who is alone when he falls, For he has no one to help him up. 11 Again, if two lie down together, they will keep warm; But how can one be warm alone? 12 Though one may be overpowered by another, two can withstand him. And a threefold cord is not quickly broken.*

Decide to build bridges where you had damaged previous relationships if you can, but more importantly, ensure you build authentic relationships henceforth.

Chapter 7

From 'Little' To 'Much'.

Exodus 23:29-30

I will not drive them out from before you in one year, lest the land become desolate and the beasts of the field become too numerous for you. Little by little I will drive them out from before you, until you have increased, and you inherit the land.

Some Bible scholars believe that anything in the region of 2.5 million to 6 million Israelites came out from Egypt during the Exodus. After forty years in the wilderness, even with the passing away of the many who died because of their unbelief etc., we can assume that the number that crossed River Jordan into the Promised Land with Joshua must have been in the millions.

In the above verses, God warned them in advance about the land He was going to give them; He said He would not drive out all the original inhabitants of that land in one year. Why? So that the land will not be desolate before them. What does that tell us? It tells us that the land was bigger and vaster than the number of people that came into it. This means that the possession they were coming into would be more than what they could completely occupy in their first year.

Every blessing that God gives you, every deposit that the Spirit of God has made into your life, every promise God has made to you, usually has the potential to be much more than your physical eyes or mind can perceive initially. Simply put, whatever you see at the beginning is only like the 'tip of an iceberg'.

I want everyone reading to begin to envision that as far as God is concerned, what He has placed in you, and planned for you, is bigger than your human eyes can see right now. "Could that be true?"

I'm glad you asked. The Bible says in 1 Cor. 2:9, that "What God has planned for people who love Him is more than eyes have seen or ears have heard. It has never even entered our minds!" (**CEV**)

I trust the Lord God will help you see that the life before you had been prepared before you arrived on the scene. If The Lord God prepared it Himself, as He rightfully says in **Jeremiah 29:11 (MSG)** "*I know what I'm doing. I have it all planned out — plans to take care of you, not abandon you, plans to give you the future you hope for*"; then, it must be an awesome life! You are not where you are by accident. You do not possess what you have, nor do you lack what you think you do not have by any accident. It is all in His original master plan for your life.

Rom 8:29 (MSG)
*God knew what he was doing from the very beginning. He decided from the outset to shape the lives of those who love him along the same lines as the life of his Son. The Son stands first in the line of humanity he restored.
We see the original and intended shape of our lives there in him.*

Before you stepped into that arena, the situation where you are today, you must realize that what God has already set before you is larger than what you are seeing. God has a reason for not giving you everything in one go.

Exodus 23:29-30 speaks of "the wild beasts". Do you know what the wild beasts are? They eat up everything you have worked for. There are blessings that you cannot afford to give to ill-prepared people. One of such is money. Everyone wants money; but you need to be mature to handle money, otherwise, it could damage you?

In this chapter, I want to attempt to unpack the process that will help you get from where you are as you read these pages to the place that you were created for, and have often dreamt to be. The word used in Exodus 23:30, referred to above, *'increased'*, simply means to grow into maturity or become fruitful. It means until you are mature or increased in number, and strength. You need to be able to withstand the enemy and drive out the 'wild beasts' that are sitting on 'your land'.

Psalms 23:5a
You prepare a table before me in the presence of my enemies...

Have you ever asked yourself, "Am I ready to eat on this table?" Not everyone has the courage to eat in the very presence of their enemies? For some, the mere sight of their enemies, even the news of them, scares them so much. It takes guts, courage, wisdom, maturity and spiritual muscles to sit - while your enemy is snarling at you, and look him in the eye and say, "You are wasting your time devil, I am eating what my Father has prepared for me."

The hope and expectation in my heart is that you will get to the point where God blesses you and nothing scares you. God will bless you little by little to possess what He has made for you.

Another tendency in us humans (and I don't think we got that from our creator, rather I think it's been induced in us by reason of the prevalent culture of our times) is to want to have it all, ***now***! And when that does not appear to happen, we fret, we become anxious, we lose our peace, we become troubled, and some even become depressed.

The plan of the enemy on this is to stress you to the point where your hands hang down, where you accept that there is really nothing ahead of you. You have been praying and waiting for so long, the miracle has not yet happened, so you think it is never going to happen again, and then you accept defeat.

You may have realized by now that whoever quits, forfeits so much more than what they have received already. It does not make sense to quit at any point in life. God says He will drive them out little by little; so your assignment is to build into yourself, tenacity; and ask for the wisdom of God to guide and help you build, handle, and process that 'little' so as to increase yourself, and enable you take another step when He gives you the next 'little'.

One of the key lessons you will learn from The Lord's outline for prayers in Matthew 6, from verse 11, is "Give us this day our daily bread". It didn't say, "Give us this year…", neither did it say, "Give us, all the days of our lives, our daily bread." The question is, why 'this day'?

The Lord wants you to trust Him for today; faith is **now**. When you move your worries into tomorrow, you are moving into an uncharted territory, and you become anxious and unnecessarily troubled, and then you begin to doubt.

Hebrews 11:1 says,

Now faith is the substance of things hoped for, the evidence of things not seen.

Faith is now. In Matthew 6:34, the Bible says,

Therefore do not worry about tomorrow, for tomorrow will worry about its own things. Sufficient for the day is its own trouble

Very few things weaken the faith of the believer like fear, anxiety and concerns (worries) about the future. I agree that the teaching on dreams and visions urges us to dream big dreams, and to plan ahead; however, it does not mean we should cease celebrating today. It actually demands that we maximize today, while we plan for tomorrow, but it does not tell us to live in tomorrow. Any teaching that tells you to live in tomorrow at the expense of today, is not worth the time you spend listening to it.

Humanly speaking, we tend to want to live in tomorrow; so, if you really ask yourself why you are worried, you probably will discover that what is troubling you has nothing to do with the thing that is before you or your life of today. Today, you could easily eat, relax and encourage somebody. Your today is sorted out but many of us do not live in it, rather, we spend it worrying about and trying to live in tomorrow.

The trouble is, tomorrow never comes, because when you get to *tomorrow,* it becomes *today.* There will always be tomorrow. Physically speaking, you can never go into tomorrow; you can only live it little by little, as each day unfolds. From now on, enjoy your today! You only have 24 hours for today.

May I ask you to personalize this whenever it happens? Ask yourself, "Is what I am worried about now, actually happening now, or am I simply scared that it might happen tomorrow?"

Consider with me, if you will, the operations of the Kingdom of God. According to the Holy Scriptures, God's ways are not our ways and in order for you and

I to live successfully as believers in Christ; we must find out how God does His things and do likewise.

And He said, "The kingdom of God is as if a man should scatter seed on the ground, 27 and should sleep by night and rise by day, and the seed should sprout and grow, he himself does not know how. 28 For the earth yields crops by itself: first the blade, then the head, after that the full grain in the head. 29 But when the grain ripens, immediately he puts in the sickle, because the harvest has come."
Mark 4:26 – 29.

What lesson can we learn from this? God's way of doing things is that you are not going to sow your seed today and receive the harvest from it the very next day. There is due process. Time is involved. After the seed is sown, all conditions being favourable (like the soil type, soil moisture, the weather conditions), first comes the blade, then the ear or head before the full crop. So, naturally, you can't plant some seed of corn, and the next day, expect that you will harvest 'corn on the cob'.

Let us imagine for a moment, that you went to your farm the next day and it was all ready for harvest, what would you think? Would you jump for joy or would you be concerned about the quality of the crops? Would you not be concerned about whether it is edible? I can imagine the myriad of thoughts that would flood your mind. Why? It is because by nature, you know that things do not work that way.

In your journey of life, some of you have had the ear, some the head and some are stepping into the full corn. But don't get so tired after the blade and begin to feel like: God, it's taking too long. He insists on the process.

When God does something at the instant, it is a miracle, but that is not the only way He does His things. There are times His process kicks in and the reason for that is, to mature and prepare us to be able to inherit what He had prepared in advance for us, because if He gives you the whole land before you are sufficiently ready, you will lose it to the 'wild beasts'.

Human Factors We Contend With.

Naturally speaking, we tend to ignore the 'little'. However, as we grow older, we get wiser. The inclination in humans, especially in this 21st Century is to ignore, minimize or abuse the 'little' that we have. To a large extent, this could be attributable to the celebrity culture of our day. Various Reality TV shows are on most channels today, and we see people become celebrities on a daily basis. Often, people are misled into thinking that there is actually no need for hard work and patience in life anymore.

Let's say, for example, I have a job but it's not my ultimate job yet, so, I'm not really happy with it. My attitude towards it is bad. By so doing, I have minimized the 'little'. I may even struggle to thank God for it, since it is not what I was expecting.

I have abused the 'little'.

God's process is, if you rejoice in that 'little', He says He will give you more. "If you are faithful in that which is little, I will give you true riches." Now, you might say, "My wages at the moment are not enough to pay my bills, so I can not support the work of the Kingdom in my local church with my tithes and offerings"; "I do not have enough to support a less privileged person in my community". I want you to know that you are clearly violating the principles of the 'little'.

The Parable Of The Talents.

Matt 25:14-30

14 "For the kingdom of heaven is like a man traveling to a far country, who called his own servants and delivered his goods to them. 15 And to one he gave five talents, to another two, and to another one, to each according to his own ability; and immediately he went on a journey. 16 Then he who had received the five talents went and traded with them, and made another five talents. 17 And likewise he who had received two gained two more also. 18 But he who had received one went and dug in the ground, and hid his lord's money. 19 After a long time the lord of those servants came and settled accounts with them. 20 "So he who had received five talents came and brought five other talents, saying, 'Lord, you delivered to me five talents; look, I have gained five more talents besides them.' 21 His lord said to him, 'Well done, good and faithful servant; you were faithful over a few things, I will make you ruler over many things. Enter into the joy of your lord.' 22 He also who had received two talents came and said, 'Lord, you delivered to me two talents; look, I have gained two more talents besides them.' 23 His lord said to him,

From 'Little' To 'Much'.

There are many lessons from this extraordinary parable which are very relevant to our discussion.

You will realize that the amount of talents each servant receives is determined by the Master. If you trust God as your Lord and personal Lord, you must be content that He loves you enough to give you what He trusts as sufficient for your life and purpose in this world.

Secondly and maybe more importantly, the commendation given by the Master on the day of reckoning was the same for the man who received five as it was for the man who received two talents.

You will observe that their master spoke the same words to the two men. It is not how much you received but what you are able and willing to accomplish with that which you have received. That's what counts more before The Lord.

If you received five talents, it means your 'little' is five talents, and if you received two, it means your 'little' is two. The ultimate is little by little, you will make it. This may not be a popular teaching since this generation wants only to hear of the miracles that happen overnight.

A child of God who really desires to know the ways of God, and who wants to grow strong in the knowledge of Him, will have to find out how God does things and be led by them.

Luke 16:10-12
He who is faithful in what is least is faithful also in much; and he who is unjust in what is least is unjust also in much. 11 Therefore if you have not been faithful in the unrighteous mammon, who will commit to your trust the true riches? 12 And if you have not been faithful in what is another man's, who will give you what is your own?

If you cannot handle the 'little' successfully, you certainly will not be able to deal with the 'much'. Mastering the challenges of turning the "little" into a success story is the training you need to stay successful with the much. Imagine you were God and you knew the beginning from the end, and the end before the beginning, and you saw that I could not handle a "little" blessing successfully; would you give me much more blessings?

Absolutely not! Why? That is because you know that it could destroy me. The love of God prevents Him from hurting you because He loves you so much. Therefore, because He sees you are not faithfully engaging the little, taking the time and pains to understand the mechanics that could turn it into a success story, He will make you to wait until you can increase; and that is what teachings like this seek to do.

The Pursuit Of More

One of the reasons we are unfaithful, or violate the success principles of the 'little' is what I call the **'undisciplined pursuit of more'**. This is the spirit of the world. In the world, it doesn't matter how much you already have, you still want to have more, even when you are not blessing anybody else. It is only enough for you and you alone.

Some people want to get more, even if it means destroying an entire nation in Africa to reap the gold, diamonds and oil; they will do it just to get more.

Let us look a little more closely at the word **'discipline'**, because the key to harnessing your 'little' to 'more' is discipline. Every champion knows the meaning and power of that word. One act of indiscipline could cause you or your team the trophy or maybe even your career.

If you are disciplined personally, you will persevere; and perseverance never fails.

Rom 5:1-5
Therefore, having been justified by faith, we have peace with God through our Lord Jesus Christ, 2 through whom also we have access by faith into this grace in which we stand, and rejoice in hope of the glory of God. 3 And not only that, but we also glory in tribulations, knowing that tribulation produces perseverance; 4 and perseverance, character; and character, hope. 5 Now hope does not disappoint, because the love of God has been poured out in our hearts by the Holy Spirit who was given to us.

But when you are not disciplined, you abuse the 'little'; your faith fluctuates; you become afraid and you think God is not at work in your life any more.

He is always at work in us. "He that keeps you neither slumbers nor sleeps". It is you and I that experience summer, so we need a holiday, but God doesn't go on holiday. The only god that goes on vacation is in Hollywood movies. The true and living God does not go on vacation, He never abandons His projects. Whatever He started, He is always sure to complete at His own time in His own way. He is God.

That means that God is committed to fulfilling His promises to you, howbeit, from step to step; from grace to grace; from glory to glory. Every day you are guaranteed to receive sufficient mercies from God for that day.

But when you allow the troubles of life, reckless pursuit for more, reckless living and the desire for more than you can handle to take over your system, you will be in danger of violating important principles of increase.

✼

Chapter 8

Self – Discipline.

A disciplined and structured person would be able to sit down and actually appreciate whatever they have today as a part of what God has put into their life for where He is taking them. He has provided for you and you have a responsibility to tend, take care of, nurture, value, and to use it the way God expects you to use it.

If you are going to fulfil the purpose of God for your life, and become what you were born to be, doing the things God has laid in your heart to do, it does not matter where you are coming from, or what you have been through. What really matters is the discipline you cultivate in your life to enable you pursue your dream.

I'm going to share with you what discipline is and what it is not. According to Dr. John Maxwell, in one of his free articles, we can learn four major things about discipline.

1
Discipline Has A Cost.

Discipline will cost you something, sometimes, everything. It demands continual investment in time, energy, and commitment at the expense of momentary pleasure and ease. Discipline means putting in hours of practice after practice for the price of skill, spending time and giving up short-term gratifications and benefits, for the hope of building yourself up to where you are going.

Discipline demands that rather than sit, worry and waste your mind on unproductive things, you actually sit down and discover what you have in the house.

The ancient prophet of God, Elisha, had to insist before the widow who was indebted, realized she had a cruise of oil in the house. As far as she was concerned, she had nothing. It takes discipline to sit down and question yourself, your processes or habits, your way of thinking, priorities and budget plans to be able to discover what is really available to you.

Recently, I read a column in a financial publication that says we can save money in so many ways. The one that really caught my attention was the revelation on how much one spends on coffee annually. (I am a coffee drinker and I enjoy my latte).

A cup of coffee, at one of the popular high street coffee joints, every morning will set one back around £2.15 for that *venti latte*. If we limit it to one cup of latte in the mornings and one in the evenings, that translates to about £4:30 spent each day on latte because it is good. Multiply that over a week and you have spent over £30 pounds. In a month, you've gone over £120. And in one year, and you would have contributed in excess of £1500 towards the high street coffee bean business.

Remember that every time you buy the latte, there is that cookie 'calling your name' and if you are not disciplined, you will also buy it? So, from 4 pounds 30 pence a day, you could actually exceed 6 pounds. I'm not trying to teach you to be thrifty, No! Be liberal in your thinking and giving, but do you know it requires discipline for you to be able to say to yourself, "Do I really need this designer handbag or that pair of shoes,"?

When a new movie is released, there are people who just cannot wait to watch it; otherwise they feel that they have missed out on what is current. There is nothing wrong with that, but sometimes, discipline will demand that you say to yourself, "Maybe I should skip some, because Hollywood producers will always produce more exciting movies every other week. So why do I have to queue up every time to watch a movie? I must discipline myself." In this day and age when the economy of the world is shrinking and cash flow is not as it used to be. You need to educate and discipline yourself in order to come out of it on top.

2
Discipline Transforms Talent Into Greatness.

One advantage of practicing personal disciple in any area of your life is that it brings you greatness. I read an article recently that pointed out the fact that if one consistently puts aside £50 or its equivalent each week into a savings account without spending anything out of it, then after 20 years, depending upon the interest rates over the period and other economic factors, you would have saved quite some money.

Has there been one month that you did not have some spare cash that you could have easily kept away? The point here is that it will take discipline to take that £20 and save it. But because we are used to spending everything we earn, sometimes before we even earn them, when a million comes into our hands, it will equally go.

Have you ever had a lump sum of money, and then it "suddenly" disappeared? Upon waking up, you could not explain just what happened to the money so quickly? What happens when you have a lump sum of money? Even after you have spent out of it, your mind still sees it as the lump sum. At the end, you'll be afraid to check your balance because you will not be happy with what you might see.

Take care of the 'little' so that you can advance to the 'much'. God's process is that He cannot release everything you need in one day. When the children of Israel cried in the desert that they needed food, God said He was going to give them manna, but that they should not take more than a daily portion.

What did some of them do? They would gather more than what they needed for the day and by the next morning, there would be maggots in what they had gathered; it would stink. Why? The Lord Jesus gave us understanding by teaching us to ask in prayers thus: **"Give us THIS DAY our daily bread"**; I want to encourage you to start practicing self-discipline. Find out the excesses that you can not afford to spend on anymore, and be disciplined enough to say, 'I'm setting this aside for something'.

It is said, "The heights by great men reached and kept, were not attained by sudden flight; but they, while their companions slept, were toiling upwards in the night". No man ever rises from the ground to the pinnacle of their lives at once; God takes you step by step. From grace to grace and from glory unto glory.

3
Discipline Majors On Choices And Not On Situations.

Discipline will enable you focus on choices, and not on the situation you may find yourself in. Bringing discipline into your life will enable you to approach your decisions, not by the way you think or feel or the conditions around you, but by the choices that will lead you forward. People that spend their time on how they feel and dwell in their thoughts on those conditions will always make the wrong decisions or choices in life.

A disciplined mind will choose between what is important and what appears urgent but not necessarily important. That alone can determine where you end up in life. I recommend that you learn to be intentional in your choices rather than be driven by the temporal conditions in which you may find yourself at the moment.

4
Discipline Does Not Give In To Feelings.

We're talking about identifying and processing your 'little' in order to be able to attain the 'much' you so desire. We are also talking about the fact that whereas God may never give you everything you need in one go; nonetheless, He has deposited something of great potential in your life.

Feelings are very fleeting by their very nature. You could feel a certain way depending on how much sleep you managed to get last night and then feel completely differently after a few hours of rest. Your feelings are bound to change with the result of your football team's weekend performance in the English Premiership match. A lot of external factors affect how we feel. Some we can control, while others we cannot. A disciplined mind will make every effort to complete the day's tasks regardless of what the game's result or weather or breaking news is.

It takes discipline to go to church every Sunday, but applying the Word of God which you heard in church in your life is the fulfilment of that discipline. Discipline will enable you cut off the things you do not need; enable you to invest in the things that you need; and it will also enable you to reassess yourself.

The Bible says that the word of God is like a mirror, which when you look at it, you see that there are specks in your eyes which need to be removed.

I want to remind you that God has truly blessed you. If you can be diligent to discover what you have, and be disciplined enough to it, in no time, you will discover what God has done in your life. As a leader, you can not afford to wait until you have a full orchestra before you pursue excellence in your music ministry.

Self – Discipline.

Be faithful in the 'little' and He will give you 'much'. If He has blessed you to play the drums, keyboard, etc. in the church, be faithful in it and you will see Him increase His grace upon you. When you pick up the microphone to sing, sing like you are from another world. When you have an opportunity to preach, do not just preach, but preach as though thousands were listening to you and their lives depended upon it.

Before you go before God in your next prayer time asking for money, stop for a moment and ask yourself, "What do I have in the house?" Go through this process, He has blessed you with so much, but you are the one wasting it because you are always waiting for the big break.

There is not one man or woman reading this book now that God has not given enough to make him or her a great person tomorrow. The question is, are you faithful with the 'little'? Is your commitment to God and worship a true reflection of what God has blessed you with? Do you live your life with an "I-don't-have-enough-and-may-never-have" mentality, or do you wake up each day saying to yourself and to The Lord, "If I perish, let me perish, because I know that you have given me this 'little' today, and I'm going to believe You for the next 'little' tomorrow."

What I am seeing now is only a tip of the iceberg; I know you are leading me somewhere. God, it is you first." The revelation to see the 'little' comes from God, but the discipline to process the 'little' comes from you. Ask God to open your eyes to see what 'little' He has given you, and to give you the discipline to process and harness it. We all need discipline in our lives.

✺

Chapter 9

The Power Of Your Decisions.

*And there was a famine in the land, beside the
first famine that was in the days of Abraham.
And Isaac went unto Abimelech king of the
Philistines unto Gerar. And the LORD appeared
unto him, and said, Go not down into Egypt;
dwell in the land which I shall tell thee of:
Sojourn in this land, and I will be with thee, and
will bless thee; for unto thee, and unto thy seed,
I will give all these countries, and I will perform
the oath which I sware unto Abraham thy father;
And I will make thy seed to multiply as the stars
of heaven, and will give unto thy seed all these
countries, and I will perform the oath which
I sware unto Abraham thy father; And I will
make thy seed to multiply as the stars of heaven,
and will give unto thy seed all these countries;*

> *and in thy seed shall all the nations of the earth be blessed; Because that Abraham obeyed my voice, and kept my charge, my commandments, my statutes, and my laws. And Isaac dwelt in Gerar:* Genesis 26:1-6

At this point, I want to take you further afield as we explore unlocking that harvest which has been dormant within you. When I speak of harvest, I want to encourage you to take your minds away from just one dimension of harvest; i.e. Money. And if you would, please step back and observe a wider view.

Take a look at your family, your ministry and purpose on earth, your community and even beyond. At this time, I would suggest you begin to ask the question, "Why am I here"? And "Lord, what is your bigger purpose for my life?" I believe every one of us should be addressing issues that go beyond the daily food we eat, the clothes we put on, the money to pay our rent or mortgage and bills.

We should, in addition to our daily needs, be addressing issues such as those that concern posterity; issues of eternal value, issues that define your purpose in life; issues that are bigger than what you think of your individual life, issues that exceed what your dream as a child had been; issues that will affect the rest of your world and leave an indelible mark, even after you have departed planet earth; and issues that rhyme with the heartbeat of God for your generation.

As your views of life and the world around you expand, so also will God's grace upon your life. When your view of life is wider, and your perspective becomes larger, then you begin to connect with the greater purposes of God, knowing that you are in the kingdom for a definite purpose.

You would have known by now that every person who calls upon Jesus as Lord and Saviour, and professes their faith in Him, must be ready for that faith to be tested. We explored this fact earlier in chapter three.

Your faith will stand trial. It will be tested to its limits. If you have not yet had yours tested, allow me to prepare you for it. No one can escape it. Witnesses will be called. Evidence will be presented. It will go through full hearing. The Jury will sit, but friend, remember when that happens, your promotion is at hand, if you refuse to quit.

The accuser of the brethren (Satan) will bring up your past, and stop at nothing in his bid to get you to doubt God and the authenticity of your faith in Him. That is when you have to make a decision based on what you know.

I call these, **seasons of contradictions.** It's night time. It's the time of famine. It's when heaven appears to be unbearably silent. It's the time when you've done all you know to do, yet nothing changes. Then what next?

Making Decisions during Moments of Contradictions.

Every one of us will come to the moment when we must confront our season of contradictions. There was a man in the book of Ruth called Elimelech. His name means 'My God is King'. He lived in Bethlehem Judah, meaning 'Land of bread'; and he got married to a woman called Naomi, meaning 'pleasant' or 'amiable'. The Bible says he had two sons- Chilion and Mahlon, and because of the famine (season of contradictions) that happened in his time; he decided to move to the land of Moab. To cut the story short, he died untimely. Every time you turn your back on God's promises due to the challenge in front of you, you walk into bigger trouble.

In contrast to Elimelech, a Moabite woman, Ruth, having lost her husband and everything else and who had no relationship or knowledge of God, and was not a part of the covenant God had with His people, said to Naomi, "Where you go, I will go; where you lodge, I will lodge; your God shall be my God." She made a decision to connect with and put her trust in the God of Israel, even in the face of extreme uncertainties. The result was that a foreigner broke through and became the great-grandmother of David and therefore, was included in the genealogy of our Lord Jesus Christ.

A stranger, a widow, had her 'faith' tested: her first husband died but she made a decision to follow God and she held on to God, even the God she did not know. At the end of time, she became the mother of Obed, and the Bible says he was the father of Jesse, and Jesse was the father of David.

Scripture often refers to Jesus as the son of David, which in a sense implies that He also was the son of Ruth. Because one woman made up her mind to either sink or swim, stand or fall, whether she knew anything or not, she was determined to obey God, and the result was that heaven had no choice but to honour her faith.

Think about it. Of all the women in Israel; of all the women of the covenant, God took one woman: a foreigner, who, because of her perseverance, became the great, great, grandmother of Jesus. Your decisions, during times of famine are vital.

Isaac Had Decisions to Make Also

In his day, Abraham encountered famine and he went into Egypt; the Bible says that he got into trouble there. Isaac, like his father, also, wanted to go to Egypt, the moment there was famine.

For those of you who are parents, I want you to understand this: your children are watching you. Your actions and decisions, especially during times of crises form an indelible foundation in the minds of your children. What they see you do in tough times, they will most likely do also. While your words are very important to them, know that your actions speak so much louder to them than you can ever imagine.

As a pastor, I have seen parents who would quite easily ignore their faith when things do not go right, and would only come back to seek God's help after they have exhausted every human option available to them.

What a shame! What are you teaching the young ones? That God comes second in life? Can you or anyone at that really afford not to seek God first in these days that we live in?

On Isaac's journey to Egypt, God met with him and told him, "Don't go down to Egypt, stay in this land and I will be with you, and I will bless you."

Consequently, Isaac made a decision to obey God and stayed where God wanted him to be. As a result, he prospered in the land and became very great, while the rest of the nation languished under the famine.

Suggestions To Consider
Before Making Major Decisions

We all know how much our decisions affect our lives and the lives of those around us. Therefore, I would like to suggest that before you make any or major decisions, you consider the following as a guidance.

Is this decision a result of any kind of fear?

Do I have all the facts I need to make this decision?

How will this decision impact my dream and my future?

Who stands to gain or lose from this decision?

Have I weighed all the factors involved and considered all the people who will be affected by this decision?

How will this decision impact on my faith in Jesus?

Can I say definitively that I prayed for God's guidance and waited for His response to me concerning this decision?

Finally, can I say clearly that this is what God wants me to do at this time?

✸

Chapter 10

Ten Practical Steps To Help Unlock Your Own Harvest.

"You can always find the sun within yourself if you will only search."
---Maxwell Maltz:

Whereas this is not meant to be a how – to – do book, all the same, I feel that I should suggest a few simple practical steps to the reader who is keen on putting the principles of this book to use, on how you could begin the process of unlocking the Harvest that is within you.

Again, I must emphasize that these suggestions are from personal experience, which I have found very useful to me in the course of my life and ministry.

Also, the steps I shall present here are by no means exhaustive, nor are they in any particular order. There has not been a specific scientific research to back them up except that I have found them successful in my life and in the lives of countless people whom I have had the privilege of mentoring and helping over the years.

Finally, they are never meant to replace the path for your life as revealed to you by The Lord who saved and called you to Himself.

Step One

In order to "unlock" that which is hidden, you have to know that it does exist indeed.

An ancient Jewish wisdom stipulates "Do not be scornful of any person, and do not be disdainful of anything, for you have no person without his hour, and you have nothing without its place."

There is really no benefit at all in expending time and resources trying to find anything if you do not "**know**" or believe that it does indeed exist.

Your live is powered by those beliefs that are core to your being. This must be right up there among your top CORE BELIEFS.

Romans 12:2 commands that we be transformed or changed by renewing our minds with God's Word which is also God's vision for us.

Changing what you believe of you will change you eternally.

Step Two

Set a realistic goal which you wish to achieve over a specific period of time.

What is the harvest you are expecting? Do not make the common mistake of trying to achieve overnight success. Faith is not presumption nor is it foolishness. Be realistic with yourself. That is not faithlessness. It is called 'wisdom'. Knowing what and where you're aiming makes it easier to hit your target. Beware not to set a timid, fear – driven goal either. A good goal should require God's help to reach and yet within the level of your faith.

Step Three

Ask yourself serious and probing questions and write down every answer you can give. Keep asking and keep reviewing the answers.

Try to write down what it is that you are good at, those things you can do almost effortlessly. Write down the things or resources that you have, such as the people you know; the places you have been; the skills or experiences you have acquired (those you consider useful and those you think were useless).

The list of questions is endless depending on your chosen field and your set of skills, experiences and knowledge.

You may not be able to properly evaluate the answers you have not written down.

Step Four

Who are your friends? Or 'Neighbours'?

These should not be limited only to the people around you. Are there people you could seek Godly counsel from? Are there people who would agree to mentor you? A good mentor would be able to see the potentials in you even before you begin to imagine it. A mentor will show you pitfalls to avoid and help you process information more clearly, because they have 'been there'.

Who can you call your friend in times like these? Approach them.

Step Five

Write down what the people around you have, that they are likely to release to you, without much ado.

What skill does your spouse possess? What of your children, parents, siblings? Your very close friends or classmates? What do they have access to which can be of benefit to you? There is no shame in asking your children, your friends or colleagues to teach you skills you do not have if they have them. What 'vessels' can you 'borrow' from your neighbour?

Step Six

Research.

When you have realised the areas you are gifted in or the things you possess, or that are available to you 'in your house', the next logical thing to do is to find out how those skills or items or connections could be turned into profit. Find out who needs such skills? How did other people who possess similar skills use theirs to improve their lives? Research into how they started, etc. You may need to visit the Library or get online now.

Step Seven

*List out your fears and prayerfully ask
The Holy Spirit to open your eyes to see
why they are not to be feared.*

Every human being contends with one fear or the other at one time or the other throughout their life time. That's a fact of life. When you succumb to any fear, you are crippled and drained of the strength to proceed in life. Winners or successful people are not people without fear but those who have realised how to defeat or master or contain their fears. In Judges 6 – 8, Gideon was afraid just like his compatriots but he was not filled with fear. The result was that God still used him. He succeeded. You too can.

Step Eight

Spend quality time in prayers and study of the Bible.

The Holy Scriptures says trust in the Lord with all your heart, in all your ways acknowledge Him and He shall direct your path. David saw the Word as a lamp unto his feet and a light unto his path. Let God speak to your heart. This will form the anchor for your ship whenever the waters become rough.

Prayers will connect the dots for you and the picture will become clearer than when you first started. Let God connect it all up for you and show you what to do with all the answers you've written down.

Step Nine

Just do it!

That's true. Just do it. Do not be afraid to start out small. The journey of a thousand miles begins with a step. You may not need all the money that you think you do not do; nor will you have all the information you think you should have at any given time. Great leaders make their decisions with anything from 40% to 70% of the information. Waiting for 100% may never happen. Don't be afraid to start small if you have to. At least you will have enough to start. DO IT.

Step Ten

Never Give Up!

This was one of Sir Winston Churchill's mantra. It is biblical. God never quits. Do not. Thomas Edison made 700 attempts before he discovered a functional Electric Bulb. Perseverance is a winning key.

✶

Chapter 11

5 Things You Should Know About Harvest

Before the reward there must be labour.
You plant before you harvest.
You sow in tears before you reap joy.
------Ralph Ransom

I trust that by now, your enthusiasm is high and you have discovered the potentials within you that are ready to be unleashed.

Before we round up, there are five important facts you should know concerning your harvest.

1
God Alone Prepares And Preserves Harvest For His People.

I recently had lunch in Dallas with a man of God who is well known worldwide. It was a unique privilege. This was a man who was blazing a trail around the world. The lunch was not just about the food, but more about the opportunity to be mentored.

A question was asked by one of the men of God present, "What was your greatest regret in ministry, now that you've reached the pinnacle, where every minister aspires to be?" He dropped his cutlery, and thought for a while and then said, "I have only one regret: and that is that I spent most of my life fighting to get to the top, only to discover on getting there, that the top was empty and slippery".

That was certainly much to swallow. But he kindly elaborated that the majority are closer to God when they are still trusting God for the breakthrough than they are when they've finally arrived. Many people tend to ascribe their success to their sheer hard work, competences, genius, connections and so on.

When they get into their harvest or when the breakthrough arrives, then they lose it. The Lord God warns His people against this very destructive complacency in Deuteronomy 8

Deut. 8:11-19

11 "Beware that you do not forget the Lord your God by not keeping His commandments, His judgments, and His statutes which I command you today, 12 lest — when you have eaten and are full, and have built beautiful houses and dwell in them; 13 and when your herds and your flocks multiply, and your silver and your gold are multiplied, and all that you have is multiplied; 14 when your heart is lifted up, and you forget the Lord your God who brought you out of the land of Egypt, from the house of bondage; 15 who led you through that great and terrible wilderness, in which were fiery serpents and scorpions and thirsty land where there was no water; who brought water for you out of the flinty rock; 16 who fed you in the wilderness with manna, which your fathers did not know, that He might humble you and that He might test you, to do you good in the end — 17 then you say in your heart, **'My power and the might of my hand have gained me this wealth.'**

18 "And you shall remember the Lord your God, for it is He who gives you power to get wealth, that He may establish His covenant which He swore to your fathers, as it is this day. 19 Then it shall be, if you by any means forget the Lord your God, and follow other gods, and serve them and worship them, I testify against you this day that you shall surely perish

---

Never forget that every harvest comes from God.

Hos 6:11
Also, O Judah, a harvest is appointed for you, when I return the captives of My people.

It is The Lord God who appoints every man's harvest, and the Almighty God has appointed your own harvest. God appoints both the time and season of every man's or Ministry's Harvest as well as the bountifulness of the harvest. The race is not to the swift.......

Jer 5:23-24
But this people have a defiant and rebellious heart; They have revolted and departed. 24 They do not say in their heart, "Let us now fear the Lord our God, Who gives rain, both the former and the latter, in its season. He reserves for us the appointed weeks of the harvest."

God can, God will and God has indeed appointed every man's time of harvest, which is the end of each season of contradictions, the end of each night time and the beginning of rest. God has appointed for you, the end of famine and the beginning of your harvest. Believers must learn to make the switch when the new day dawns. Faith and spiritual perception is essential.

2 Sam 5:12 (KJV)
And David perceived that the Lord had established him king over Israel, and that he had exalted his kingdom for his people Israel's sake.

After years of dwelling in desserts and caves and fleeing from the armies of King Saul, just to stay alive. After running from one cave to the next wilderness, King David came to the day when he 'perceived' or just 'knew within his heart' that famine was over. His season of appointed harvest had arrived.

You must discern it for yourself or no one may tell you. The Bible says that He opens and no man can shut, and He shuts and no man can open. When God says that the appointed time for your blessing has come, no force on the face of the earth can change it; they may fight but they will not prevail.

2
Harvest Time Is Not The Time To Rest.

I was studying on this subject recently when The Lord spoke this to me. He asked me, "***Do you know that the enemy tricks many people successfully at the time of their harvest? They drop their hands, and lower their guard, and think that it is their time to rest***"

Have you ever observed some people go from struggles to harvest and very soon, they are back to struggles, and soon again, they are back up and before you cold see the fruits of the harvest, they are down again. This is not the will of God for His children. No! God wants you blessed and He wants you to be a blessing. There is, however, a key principle God showed to me. That is, harvest time is not the time to rest.

Prov 6:6-11
Go to the ant, you sluggard! Consider her ways and be wise, 7 Which, having no captain, Overseer or ruler, 8 Provides her supplies in the summer, **And gathers her food in the harvest.** *9 How long will you slumber, O sluggard? When will you rise from your sleep? 10 A little sleep, a little slumber, A little folding of the hands to sleep — 11 So shall your poverty come on you like a prowler, And your need like an armed man.*

When your field is ready for harvest, you shouldn't be resting; it's time to go in and put in the sickle.

Joel 3:13
Put in the sickle, for the harvest is ripe…….

Several years ago, my friend and I were to go for a Bible study meeting and I told him that I wanted to sleep a little; he then opened this scripture to me. I was reading from his Bible and immediately I threw off my pyjamas and said, "God forbid it." For those who prefer to sleep when they should be praying, please note this. In Proverbs 10:5,

---

Prov 10:4-5
He who has a slack hand becomes poor, But the hand of the diligent makes rich. 5 He who gathers in summer is a wise son; He who sleeps in harvest is a son who causes shame.

This shows us very vividly that harvest time is not really the time to sleep. Now, what is sleep? I'm not talking about the eight hours that you need in the night. There are people who have the luxury of twelve to thirteen hours of sleep daily, and they still want to sleep a little more. The enemy tells you to sleep just a little more, even when the alarm clock has gone off. The devil knows that a little more sleep, and you could lose your job.

The Message Translation of this scripture says, **"Harvest time is not the time to go fishing or to live in pleasure."**

In my Pastoral ministry, I have laid hands on many people and seen God really prosper them. Some of them are still in faith, but what disheartens me deeply is that some of them are no longer in the faith. Then I said, "Lord, why?" And He said to me, "It is because they went to sleep in harvest."

Take for instance, if you are in business and God opens a door for you to make a million pounds in profit. You may decide, "I have always wanted to go to Hawaii, and I have also been longing to cruise the Caribbean", while the business that brought the million pounds is still to be executed. That is slumber and sleep.

Let me read to you from the Contemporary English Version:

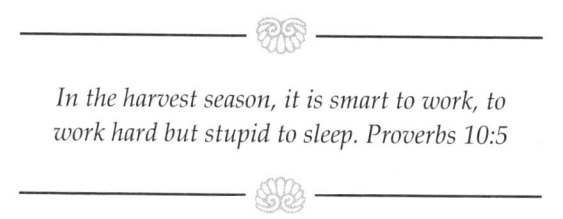

In the harvest season, it is smart to work, to work hard but stupid to sleep. Proverbs 10:5

When I read that, I realized why our lives seem to go up and then, only to go back down again. What does it mean to sleep? It is to take your ease when you are, actually, supposed to be working. To reduce the commitment with which you fought your way to the top.

The same, if not more, fervency that brought you harvest is required during harvest, so as to guarantee the next harvest. If you were fasting, praying and sowing seeds, and you step into your harvest, why do you stop? When you were in need, you were all over God, anything God wanted done, you were more than available to do it. Then, suddenly, the first blessing, the first shoots begin to arrive in your life, and you are too busy to do anything for God.

If you were sowing seeds for harvest, when the harvest comes, sow more seeds. The fact of the harvest in itself gives you more seeds to sow and much more food to eat. Whatever it is you were doing before your harvest started, don't stop, rather, do more.

Luke 12:47-48 (MSG)
"The servant who knows what his master wants and ignores it, or insolently does whatever he pleases, will be thoroughly thrashed. 48 But if he does a poor job through ignorance, he'll get off with a slap on the hand. Great gifts mean great responsibilities; greater gifts, greater responsibilities!

3
Harvest Time Is Also Judgment Time.

"Nearly all men can stand the test of adversity, but if you really want to test a man's character, give him power ---------Abraham Lincoln

The Parable of the Wheat and the Tares

Matt 13:24-30
Another parable He put forth to them, saying: "The kingdom of heaven is like a man who sowed good seed in his field; 25 but while men slept, his enemy came and sowed tares among the wheat and went his way. 26 But when the grain had sprouted and produced a crop, then the tares also appeared. 27 So the servants of the owner came and said to him, 'Sir, did you not sow good seed in your field? How then does it have tares?' 28 He said to them, 'An enemy has done this.' The servants said to him, 'Do you want us then to go and gather them up?' 29 But he said, 'No, lest while you gather up the tares you also uproot the wheat with them. 30 Let both grow together until the harvest and at the time of harvest I will say to the reapers, "First gather together the tares and bind them in bundles to burn them, but gather the wheat into my barn."'"

The need for you to remain fervent in harvest is further emphasized by the fact that harvest time is also judgment time. Harvest time is a time of blessing, celebration, testimonies, etc., but it is also a time when God is watching what fruit you are producing. The true colour of the human heart comes out when they have food to eat and clothes to wear and some change in their pockets.

Wheat and tares are both wheat except that tares are of the wild stock. They both look alike, flower alike but "by their fruits you shall know them". The Lord blesses His people and wants them to show it.

Dr. C. H. Spurgeon once commented that it was sin to cover up God's blessings in the guise of modesty. When God has blessed you, show it. Remember that God's blessings will also show you off. What is the true state of your heart?

4
Seedtime Always Preceeds Harvest

Gen 26:12-16
Then Isaac sowed in that land, and reaped in the same year a hundredfold; and the Lord blessed him. 13 The man began to prosper, and continued prospering until he became very

> *prosperous; 14 for he had possessions of flocks and possessions of herds and a great number of servants. So the Philistines envied him. 15 Now the Philistines had stopped up all the wells which his father's servants had dug in the days of Abraham his father, and they had filled them with earth. 16 And Abimelech said to Isaac, "Go away from us, for you are much mightier than we."*

A careful examination of Genesis 26 will reveal the following among the many other truths embedded therein:

- It was God's idea and specific instruction to Isaac to stay in the land even though the land was experiencing famine at the time.
- God knew of the famine in the land
- God specifically told Isaac that He would bless Isaac in that land despite the famine.
- Isaac believed God and demonstrated it by obeying His commands. He remained in the land Gerar.

If I were Isaac, I would have simply gone to bed awaiting the fulfilment of the divine promise of providence. After all God can not lie! But Isaac did something he was not told to do, at least from the text available to us here.

Or could Isaac have learnt this powerful revelation from his father Abraham? Even though he knew that God said He would bless him, Isaac knew there had to be something that would activate the blessing. You have to release something to activate the promised blessing.

Eccl 11:4 says:
He who observes the wind will not sow, And he who regards the clouds will not reap.

Also

Prov. 12:10 says:
He who tills his land will be satisfied with bread, But he who follows frivolity is devoid of understanding.

That is why even though God told Isaac He would be with him, and bless him, Isaac sowed in that land. Why did he have to sow in that land? It is because it was the land he fed from and lived in. That is why I said that there is a principle of life about sowing and reaping.

Every human being knows that in order to reap from a field, somebody must of necessity; have to drop some seed into that field.

There will come a time in your life when you will come into the realization that God has given you a specific promise; maybe you were studying the scriptures and the Holy Spirit ignites your faith to receive a particular promise, or a prophetic declaration is made under the unction of the Holy Spirit over your life. The day you accept that promise, it becomes yours, but what has to happen to activate it in your life is that you have to be ready to exchange something in order to connect it into your life.

I am very much aware of the indifference or suspicions that greet the message of sowing and reaping in the church. This is largely due to the excesses that many teachers of the Word have introduced to adulterate the truth of scripture for their selfish gains. That notwithstanding, child of God, the principles that the Almighty God Himself has laid down to govern the earth and human existence can never be broken.

Two people, one a king, the other a prince with God's promise, in the same land, going through the same famine; or if you removed their titles, you could say two people: one knew the principles of life, while the other did not. The one that did not know the principle of life survived, endured, struggled and coped with the famine, but the one that knew the principles of life, knew that the way out of the famine was to sow seeds.

Isaac sowed that year and God prospered him, and he sowed again. This was because he knew that every time he sowed, he would reap; and when the harvest comes, he would sow some more. The king and his men came to Isaac and told him that the land was not large enough for the both of them, and soon, Isaac became so prosperous that he would have taken over the entire land, but he was asked to leave the land.

5
Continuous Sowing Guarantees Continuous Harvest.

"Even after a bad harvest there must be sowing"
-------Lucius Annaeus Seneca

The Lord God spoke to Noah, upon receiving Noah's sacrifice after the flood, during which time He promised never to destroy the Earth again with water,

While the earth remains, seedtime and harvest, and cold and heat, and summer and winter, and day and night shall not cease.
Genesis 8:22

This is a very important principle that many have not taken the time to learn well enough and to practice. Notice here that the Lord God Almighty states for the benefit of mankind, four cycles which shall never cease as long as we remain upon the earth. As long as we observe seedtime, harvest is guaranteed. As long as cold comes and keeps coming, heat is guaranteed to follow. The same goes for summer and winter and Day and Night.

God never intends for our harvest to cease but the key is in the details. Your seedtime must never cease either! For continuous harvest, you must maintain continuous seedtime or sowing.

Eccl 11:5-6
As you do not know what is the way of the wind, Or how the bones grow in the womb of her who is with child, So you do not know the works of God who makes everything. 6 **In the morning sow your seed, And in the evening do not withhold your hand;** *For you do not know which will prosper, Either this or that, Or whether both alike will be good.*

The cycle must never be broken if continuous harvest is to be guaranteed.

Do you need joy in your life, then look out and maybe even ask God to show you folks into whose lives you could sow seeds of joy.

Do you trust God for a godly partner and a relationship that will last your lifetime? Sow seeds of intercession into the lives of couples you know.

Do you trust God for your own children? How about stepping out and sparing a few hours to babysit for a young couple so they could go watch a movie together or whatever they might choose to do with that rare spare time?

How about volunteering just a little more in your local church or maybe helping out at your church office with some administrative work? Be a continuous blessing to others and see God's blessings flow ceaselessly into your life.

This is not just about money, it's about sowing of your time, your skills, your talents, your smiles or whatever God has blessed you with.

It is about choosing to be a blessing to other people, and giving out whatever you have as a seed to bless others. As you do this continuously, God can never abandon you and your harvest will never cease.

✳

Chapter 12

Last Word.

It is my sincere hope that having read this book to this point; you have been encouraged to begin the journey of discovering the vastness of the riches of God's deposits in your life.

Mankind is the finest specie of God's creation. The ultimate of God's creation. In Ephesians, Apostle Paul refers to us as God's Masterpiece, created in Christ Jesus for good works. That's exactly what we are, especially those of us who are in Christ.

However, as a believer in Christ, I am increasingly troubled by the current trend exploding in the Body of Christ. It would appear to me that financial prosperity and general well-being, more than anything else, is the primary motivation in the minds of many people who attend churches these days.

While this is not the case everywhere, it is clearly so in many communities and nations today. The result is that shallow Christians are commonplace. Many have no accurate knowledge of what the Bible says, except for the regular 'christianese' that is regularly being spoken in their churches.

Consequently, most believers today are quite easily swayed by fads and 'new things', many of which are so superficial, that one wonders why people still patronize them.

While I do not have any problem with our prospering and being in health, I am concerned that it is fast replacing the need for a life worthy of our calling as Christians. The Holy Scripture still demands of us to contend for the faith that was once delivered unto the saints.

I urge you to rediscover the joy of purposeful in-depth Bible studies and spending time in the secret place of prayer. Draw near to God and He will draw near to you.

Jesus did not need to die for God's people to prosper. Abraham, Isaac, King David, King

Solomon; just to name a few old testament saints, prospered exceedingly before the incarnation of the Son of God.

Moses, by lifting up the brazen serpent in the wilderness, brought healing to God's people before Jesus came on the scene.

Those who only sought the hand of God all perished in the wilderness while the man, Moses, who was content to seek the face of God left an enduring legacy.

I trust that as you apply the principles discussed in this book, you will remember what Matthew 16:26 27 has to say!

Matt 16:26-27
26 For what profit is it to a man if he gains the whole world, and loses his own soul? Or what will a man give in exchange for his soul? 27 For the Son of Man will come in the glory of His Father with His angels, and then He will reward each according to his works.

Your Soul Is Priceless.

The greatest assurance a child of God should have must be the certainty that should the trumpet sound tonight, they would make it to the marriage super of the Lamb.

Jesus is coming back for the Harvest of the Earth – the souls of men.

Scripture teaches that He has His reward with Him. You should endeavour to not only believe God for your physical life's needs, but also trust Him to help you discover His purpose for your life and strive to fulfil it while you still can.

There are many people you see every day at your workplace, at school, at the shopping mall who are in desperate need of Jesus. The Master expects them to be among the harvest He is coming for.

As we close, please allow me to share two of my favourite Scriptures with you

---

Prov 11:30
The fruit of the righteous is a tree of life, And he who wins souls is wise.

Dan 12:3
Those who are wise shall shine Like the brightness of the firmament, And those who turn many to righteousness Like the stars forever and ever.

Think about these powerful words. These have driven many like you to forsake all and pursue the calling of God on their lives for their generation.

What would you be willing to do for the sake of God's Kingdom?

The Lord Jesus is coming soon. Maranatha!